True Ghost S

30 Paranormal Tales from Arou...

Stories originally published on <u>ghostsnghouls.com</u>

True Ghost Stories: 30 Paranormal Tales from Around the World

Copyright ® 2015 Christy Gordon

Love, thieves, and fear make ghosts. - German Proverb

Introduction

The stories you are about to read come from real people from all walks of life: nurses, police officers, soldiers, teenagers, senior citizens, middle-aged men and women, and more. Everyone has a story. You just have to listen. Happy haunted reading!

The Possession

When I was serving in Thailand during the Vietnam War, I was stationed in a little town on the Thai-Laos-Cambodian border. I was living with my soon-to-be wife in a bungalow in town when our neighbor, a Laotian girl, became possessed by an evil spirit. She was so bad they had to call in special monks in white robes to pray over her. My girlfriend wanted to go over and see the exorcism, but before she went she told me not to come over for any reason.

Since I was on a day off, I sat on my porch drinking whiskey and getting drunk. In those days, there wasn't much else to do. Later, one of my girlfriend's friends came by and asked for her. Forgetting what my girlfriend had said, I went over to the exorcism house.

I went up the steps to the upper floor bungalow, walked up to the screen door, and looked inside. The girl, who was standing naked on her bed screaming, suddenly stopped yelling and pointed to the door. "There it is," she screamed in perfect English!

I was standing with my face to the screen door when I suddenly felt as if my face was in a freezer. I sensed something standing there looking at me. The hackles rose on my neck and arms, and my girlfriend, who was sitting just inside the door, screamed, "Run!"

To this day, I know something left the possessed girl to take a look at me. I was stone cold sober when I got back across the street. This happened in Korat, Thailand in 1969. I had a lot of strange things happen to me in the three years I was in Thailand.

MOP 13

Guantanamo Bay Naval Base, or GTMO, is full of ghost stories. There are stories of refugees losing their lives crossing the mine fields and stories of soldiers who never left their posts. I didn't think much of the tales until I experienced something strange one night.

I was in a Marine Observation Post, or MOP as we called them. It was MOP 13. In this post, you had to climb up a long stretch of stairs and enter through a hatch in the floor. The post was really remote and near the mine fields. It was always very dark and required night vision goggles to see anything beyond five feet. Mop 13 was a popular post because it was impossible for senior Marines to sneak up on you and catch you doing something stupid.

One night, around 9 p.m. or so, I was in MOP 13 looking into the darkness when I heard footsteps coming up the metal stairs. I remember thinking how weird it was because I didn't hear or see my staff sergeant's vehicle pull up. I figured he was trying to be sneaky and catch me sleeping.

I clearly heard the footsteps and a knock on the hatch signaling me to open the door. However, when I opened the hatch nobody was there. Needless to say, I was freaked out. I guess it could have been a dream, but I'm not sure. If it was, it was the most vivid dream I've ever had.

The Thing with No Face

While serving in the Philippine Marine Corps, I was deployed in the south of the country, to a place that has seen countless battles. I was initially assigned administrative work at our battalion HQ but was rotated to a company that was often on patrol. It was on one of these patrols that I saw something that still weakens my knees even to this day.

We often received intelligence reports of enemy sightings. This time, my squad was ordered to verify the sightings. The patrol set off for three days of humping in the bush, following leads and updating reports.

It was the second day of our patrol when intelligence came in saying that the enemy had moved out and was possibly heading to another island. We were ordered to report back to company HQ. As it was already evening when we got the report, our squad leader decided to pass the night in the bush and move out early the next morning.

We were setting perimeter when one of us spotted a faint figure about 70 yards away. Only our squad leader had night vision goggles, but he had difficulty locating the figure so he sent two fire teams downrange. I was in one of the fire teams.

The figure was quite visible even with only the moon illuminating the otherwise pitch-black surroundings. As we slowly approached and got to around 50 yards, I noticed the figure seemed to be gliding rather than moving. I thought it was strange. Closing in at around 20 yards, we saw that the figure was not only gliding, it was actually floating about two feet off the ground. It was gliding erratically, sometimes passing close to our crouched bodies. By this time I was really scared. My heart was beating so fast I thought it would pop out of my chest. What made it worse was that we all saw the figure.

It was dressed like a normal living person, but it had no face. It's as if the face was "erased." Its skin was very pale, as if drained of blood. It seemed to have bullet holes across its chest. At one point, it stopped gliding. I looked through my rifle scope, and I had the fright of my life when I saw it looking back at me with its featureless face. Every hair on my body stood up, and I had to fight the urge to run and scream. Suddenly, the figure just vanished in front of us. I think every one of us was too scared to move. We were eventually ordered to withdraw and return to the perimeter. How I didn't soil my trousers is beyond me.

We reported to our squad leader what we saw, and he said he believed us. He ordered us to prepare to move out as he radioed for transport. Everyone was quiet in the truck on the way back to company HQ. No one spoke a word. We later found out that each of us who were sent downrange had felt whatever it was look at us. Our squad leader ordered us to keep the experience to ourselves. I was silent about this until I got out of the military.

Squadron Spirit

When I was younger, I was part of the air cadets. I was often at the squadron (the place in which we'd meet for our weekly meetings) until late. One night, my stepfather asked me to go through to the next building, which was connected to the first building by a hallway, and photocopy some documents. The other building was closed as it was about 11:30 p.m., so the lights were all turned off. However, there was enough light for me to see where I was going.

As I turned the corner, I saw a very tall man in uniform walk down the corridor and into the room I was heading to. I walked into the room, turned on the light, smiled, and said "Good evening, sir," but no one was there.

I finished what I needed to do and left. As we were closing up the squadron for the night, I asked if the officer I'd seen had left the building yet. I was worried he'd get locked in. The staff looked at me, confused, and said that no one was in the building. In fact, it been closed for a few days. They checked the building, and indeed there was no one inside. After I told my stepdad what I had seen, he told me that the building was known for being haunted. They didn't tell the teenagers as they thought we might get scared.

The man I saw was a completely black, solid figure. That's why I'm sure it wasn't my mind playing tricks on me. After that experience, if I was left alone in one of the rooms at the squadron, weird stuff would happen like things falling over or loud banging noises. I believe that whoever, or whatever, is at the squadron knows that I know about him.

The Land is Cursed

I enlisted in the French Foreign Legion at the age of 19. I was a young corporal at the time this happened, in the 2nd Foreign Parachute Regiment. Now, maybe we were delusional from the extremely cold conditions and our aching feet, but we all remember what we saw and experienced that night.

Our unit was advancing through a landscape of mountains with dense forest and snow. We found a small footpath leading through the mountains which the lieutenant thought would be the best trail to follow. After following the path, we got to a kind of clearing, an open part that almost reached the pinnacle of the mountain. Nearby was a small hut, not far from the path. The lieutenant sent three men, including me, to investigate the hut while the rest of the regiment waited on the trail.

We knocked on the door and a very old man who was native to the area opened it. He looked very tired which wasn't surprising considering it was night. One of the men was a translator and asked the old man in his native language if he had seen anyone else pass by on the path. The old man claimed that no one used the path except him. He said the path further down was denser, and that the land was cursed. He then closed the door and told us to leave. We informed the lieutenant, and his orders were to keep moving.

The old man was right. The forest got increasingly dense until the trees surrounded the path on both sides. The man walking in front of me turned around and asked what I had just said. Confused, I denied saying anything. He insisted that I had just whispered something to him, and he told me to stop playing around. I know for a fact I didn't say anything, and neither did any of the other men. Suddenly, the lieutenant turned around and told us to stop whispering, but all of the men denied whispering or talking. That's common sense when you're moving through hostile territory.

Then the weird stuff started to happen. Someone, or something, suddenly started throwing stones from the right side of the tree line. The lieutenant shouted and warned whoever it was to stop, but it only got worse. The stones flew at us from both sides. Weird laughter and screams came from all over. A stone hit one of the men directly in the face. Armed soldiers were being made fools of by idiots with stones. That was the final straw. The lieutenant shouted "Vérifiez vos flancs!" (Check your flanks). He then told us to advance and spread out among the trees. Now, one could say it was kids or local idiots throwing the rocks, but I could feel evil. We all could.

As we moved deeper into the trees, I saw figures moving very fast among them. They were dark figures that looked like men. A guy a few feet away from me started praying in Spanish. The lieutenant fired two shots in the air, and the sounds and stones stopped. There was complete silence. We kept following the trail until we got to where we needed to be. None of the men really spoke of the incident again.

There may be a lot of explanations, but no man moves as fast as those figures in the woods, nor can men make sounds like that. Maybe the old hermit wasn't lying, maybe the land is cursed. None of us had ever experienced anything like that, nor have we experienced anything like that since. Next time, we'll listen.

Something Wicked This Way Comes

I am an avid fisherman. I live way out in Southern Illinois, in the middle of nothing surrounded by nowhere. Because of this, I am afforded the opportunity to fish whenever I want, which is normally every day after work, minus the bitterly cold winter months. I typically fish a strand of remote ponds on Ten Mile Creek.

One afternoon in May 2013, I was at one of my favorite spots. I'd been there about 20 minutes, give or take, when I started to feel unnaturally uneasy. I can't really put into words the paranoid, gut-wrenching feeling that came over me. Now, please keep in mind, I have been doing this type of thing my whole life. I'm often by myself, deep in the woods, and until then I never experienced this urgent need to flee.

I was reeling in my line when I began to hear leaves rustling. Problem was, there was no breeze, and it had been raining the whole day up until an hour before. I immediately assumed it was a deer or a raccoon rustling nearby. However, what I saw absolutely baffled me. I witnessed a single mass of leaves rolling around along the ground. It was just to the right of my position, no more than a hundred yards.

I watched in awe as the unnatural-looking mass began to make its way across the bank. This particular pond was inset, like a bowl in the ground. There was an inlet directly to the south, at the end of the pond, and that's where I was, basically standing on the handle of a giant ladle. This mass was around 8 ft. x 8 ft. and moving southbound, just east of my location. I was frozen in fear and in absolute disbelief. The uneasy feeling quickly turned into full-blown panic.

I was trying to move, trying to get the hell out of there, but felt held in place by a feeling of utter sadness. It was by far the darkest, coldest, most empty feeling I've ever known. I then heard a horrible, guttural noise. To this this day, the noise still causes me to wake up in cold sweats. I have nightmares. I tore my gaze away from the mass long enough to snatch an AR-15 from the ATV. Until that time, I had never, ever fired my weapon at something I could not identify. I said "God, forgive me," and then fired seven rounds at the mass. However, I don't believe the shots I fired had any effect. The sound of the shots and my adrenaline did rally me enough to jump up and hurry home.

I haven't been back to the spot, though I have looked down from atop the road a few times. Before that day, I couldn't imagine anything that would keep me away from my favorite fishing hole, or terrify me that much. I'm still even sure was real. But I'll never go back there again.

Camp Terror

This happened when I was a camp counselor and canoe instructor at a kids' camp in central Ontario, Canada in the late 80s. A couple of things to know about me: I am a very experienced outdoorsman, and I don't scare easily. Even at the time of this story, I'd already spent many nights alone in the wilderness. I know what sounds the woods make and what animals do what. What we experienced was nothing natural.

Our camp was on an island in a very big lake with many rivers coming in and out and several portages to other lakes. While planning a three-day trip for my campers, I asked about one camp site near a dam and was told by the trip director that the site was closed. The reason? Two summers prior, a group from the only other camp on the lake went there and tragically lost a camper. A boy of about 11 drowned at the top of the dam when the counselors weren't watching. Tragic. Nonetheless, I wanted to take my group there and was told I could as long as we didn't let the kids swim near the dam. Done deal.

We arrived at the site on the last day of our trip. It had been very stormy for two days, but the weather had settled and there was no wind, although the sky was completely overcast.

There were a few strange things that happened during the day, such as a towel and t-shirt disappearing from a clothesline near the tent site. They somehow ended up in the water at the top of the dam several meters away, even though there was no wind. I had to swim down to retrieve the items twice, and I admit it crossed my mind while I was at the bottom that this may well have been where the boy's body ended up.

At dusk, we were gathered around the campfire. It was not yet fully dark, and we were washing up and tidying the campsite before settling in front of the fire to pass the rest of the evening. Our group consisted of two 17-year-old counselors and eight 12-year-old boys. We were laughing and horsing about when we first heard it. The sound stopped everyone in their tracks.

If you've ever heard a big tree fall in the forest, it does indeed make a sound. A really loud one. The trees pop and crack so loud, that at first you wonder if it's gunshots. That's what we heard. The evening was completely still with not even a breeze, but somewhere nearby (I would have guessed within 50 feet of our site) a big-ass tree fell. It took about 10 seconds, and we heard every part of it, right until it hit the ground. When a big tree falls, you can feel the earth shake and shudder. I've logged trees before, and this one sounded close. But apart from the sound, we saw and felt nothing.

Everyone was terrified. My buddy was craving a cigarette so bad he was useless, and he had the same look on his face as the kids. I decided to try and be cool about it and told everyone that it was likely a bear pushing over a dead tree in search of grubs.

"Let's build up the fire and make some noise, and it will scare him away," I said.

So we did. We sang, we banged pots and pans, and after 45 minutes everyone was calm. Then it happened again. However, this time the sound was much farther off, perhaps a quarter-mile away. Everyone looked at me for reassurance, and I said, "See? We're good. It's moving off." We were still mighty unsettled, but somewhat reassured that it did seem to be moving farther away.

We all relaxed and the evening wore on. About an hour later, it happened again. This time the sound was so close to where we were standing that I felt like a tree was going to fall on top of us. It was right beside me, but I saw nothing. Every pop and crack pierced our ears, and I fully expected a tree to fall right on top of us, but nothing happened. We heard it, but we again saw nothing. Everyone stood frozen in terror, looking for me to give the call to flee and looking like they might just kill me if I didn't. My own fear finally took over, and I couldn't hold it together anymore.

"Okay," I said. "Let's get out of here."

In a flash, everyone was gone down the short path leading to the boats, including the other counselor. I had meant, "Let's pack up and do this orderly," but no such luck. One kid had stayed behind with me, so together we put out the fire and did a quick sweep of the place. We then went down to the waters' edge to find the canoe they had left for us. We paddled out into the channel and found the others rafted up and waiting. The first question I asked was, "Who has a life jacket on?".

No one did. Not one person. Not even the other counselor. I was already unsure if I was going to keep my job for paddling at night, but the idea of paddling across a big lake at night without life jackets was a guaranteed "end of summer" for both of us, never mind the obvious peril.

Looking at everyone's faces, I realized I was the only one who would go back there. Fuck. I had the one camper in my canoe, so he climbed into another boat and I paddled back alone. They were so terrified they wouldn't even give me the flashlight.

Once I hit the woods, it was the kind of dark that is the same with your eyes open or closed. I started up the short trail to where the tents were. I fully admit that I was terrified, but I knew I had to do fetch the life jackets. I remember talking out loud as I wandered toward the site.

"Okay, whatever you are. I guess if you're going to get me, you're going to get me. But I need these life jackets, and I need to keep these kids safe."

In retrospect, I knew what, or who, was doing all this, and maybe I was pleading my case a bit, hoping for mercy. I also felt a bit of responsibility and talked to "him" in the way I would talk to one of my campers. Perhaps that made a difference.

My plan was to find my way to my tent, as I knew I'd left my flashlight sitting in front of it. Without that, I'd never find the lifejackets or the path back down to the water. However, this proved to be unnecessary. I'm not sure if this is coincidence, but somehow, in the complete darkness, right after I said that, I took one or two steps and found all the life jackets piled together right at my feet.

I'm an organized trip leader, and I like a clean campsite. However, I recall that we were having a lazy day and things were a bit disheveled. I hadn't put all the life jackets in a pile. Nonetheless, the very first thing I found in the pitch-black darkness was the pile of life jackets. Counting the life jackets as I picked them up, I found every last one and was back at my boat a minute later. That still amazes me.

We paddled back across the lake at night and made it to the main camp safely. Everyone made fun of us, although no one had an explanation. They said we were lying and wouldn't let it go. I can't blame them. It was terrifying because we were at the beginning of a summer in which everyone would be going out to the woods repeatedly.

I went on to become a full instructor and trip guide. I've done epic trips since then, but never experienced the sounds again. I've asked every old salt, park ranger, and aboriginal Canadian I've met about the experience. The only people who aren't completely stumped by it are the aboriginals. Their answer is simple:

"That was an angry spirit. You're lucky you were respectful to it."

The last detail to add is that we went back the next day to retrieve the gear that we had left behind, but there was not one tree down...absolutely nothing to indicate that even a single tree had fallen the night before.

The Vanishing Hunter

About 25 years ago, a friend of mine and I were out hiking one afternoon, along with his dog. We were headed to our usual campsite to see what shape it was in after the winter.

The area we were in had long had a reputation for odd occurrences, and we'd had our share over the years. Even so, it was an annual ritual to get away to "our spot" at least three or four times between Memorial and Labor Day.

It was just past noon, and we decided to break for lunch in a clearing about halfway to the campsite. We built a small fire, cooked some grub, and made coffee. The dog, after having his lunch, stretched out on the ground for a nap.

As we relaxed, drinking coffee and smoking cigarettes, the dog suddenly sat up and looked back the way we'd come. Sure enough, a figure was approaching us through the trees, a tall man dressed head to foot in camo. We didn't think much about it. That time of year (late May in Ohio), the woods were full of people hiking, fishing, and what not.

The man got to the edge of the clearing, about 20 feet from where we sat, and vanished. He'd looked solid, and real, although we later realized he'd made no sound coming down the path, nor did he appear to notice us.

The dog yawned, laid back down, and went back to sleep. We looked at each other, shrugged, and finished our coffee.

The Unseen Passenger

I had a call one day that really sticks with me. As police officers, we had a woman that we'd visited plenty of times for every complaint in the book. Well, one night we got called to her apartment after she complained of back pain.

On our arrival, she said that the pain had been going on for months, but that the "people in her room" told her not to call. The thing is, she lived alone. She also said that they could see me, but that they didn't like me because I was helping her.

I had my captain look around the apartment to make sure there wasn't anyone around and that the scene was safe. It was empty. Then, during the transport, she looked over to the empty seat next to her and said "Oh, that looks terrible. What happened to you? Well, I'm so sorry. I'm glad you aren't in pain anymore." Then she turned to me and said, "He's scary looking." She didn't know that a few hours prior, we had been called to a fatal, and really gruesome, car vs. semi-truck accident.

Come to find out, the woman had stage four brain cancer, and she passed away that night. To this day, I still wonder what she saw. Who was riding in the squad with me and my partner?

Paranormal Call

This happened in the 1980s when I was an officer with the Oklahoma City Police Department.

One week I noticed that several officers had *Ghost Busters* stickers stuck to the windows of their cars. I was confused and asked one of the guys what was with all the *Ghost Busters* stuff. He told me that a few officers had been on a freaky call recently where the occupants had complained of paranormal activity.

I wasn't there, but my buddy said that when the officers arrived at the house, the residents were outside, terrified, while the sounds of banging doors and shattering glass came from inside the house. The officers thought an intruder was inside so they brought a canine, Red, to help clear the property.

Now, Red was the meanest damn dog you ever saw, but he absolutely refused to go inside the home. He growled and whined but would not set a paw inside. Eventually, the crashing and banging noises stopped and a few officers went inside. Everything inside the home was destroyed, but there were no intruders around. The residents claimed the sounds had suddenly started up when they were inside and had no idea what caused them.

That story always gave me the creeps. None of the guys ever really talked about what happened because they were afraid everyone would think they were crazy.

The Shooter

I had just started my second year as an Oregon state trooper. I was riding with another officer when dispatch came on and said there was a call of a man holding a gun to a woman's head, so of course we got there as fast as we could.

When we arrived, we found a woman crying and repeating over and over, "He shot me. He shot me." I bent down to talk to her and said "He didn't shoot you," but she wouldn't listen. I asked if she had any family she could stay with, and she said no. She wouldn't let us take her anywhere, so we asked if she would be okay by herself. She said yes, and we left.

At the end of our night shift, we went back to the station and told the dispatcher and other officers about the weird call. An officer looked up her name and went pale. He then hesitantly told us that a young woman by that name had been shot in the head by her husband about six years ago. Police never caught the shooter. We all went grim and tried to forget about what happened. We eventually did...until two years later.

The Warning

I'm still a state cop in Oregon, but I've been promoted to K-9 handler. One day, I had just pulled over a man for speeding, but as I walked up to his window I instantly got a bad feeling about him. So, I went back to my squad car.

As soon as I got in, I felt a breeze and heard my passenger door shut. I looked up and saw a female officer, no older than myself, sitting in the passenger seat. I hadn't called for backup, and when I looked around I didn't see another squad car. There's no way she could have walked over or been in the guy's car without me noticing.

My dog Sargent was snapping and barking and growling at the woman, and the hair on his back was standing up. "Hello," I said. "Can I help you?" She said, "He has a gun by his seat." I turned to make sure the man was still in his vehicle, and when I looked back the officer was gone.

I got out, grabbed the guy from his car, and handcuffed him. I found the gun under the seat where she said it was. When I ran the man's record, I learned that he'd killed a young cop 20 years ago. I took him in, and he was eventually sentenced to life in prison.

Later that night, I was playing ball with Sargent when the officer appeared again. "Thank you," I said. "No, thank you," she replied. I told her she'd saved my life, and she said "I was only doing my job. He would have killed you with the same gun he used to kill me." After that, she disappeared.

I have never personally seen the woman again, but there are new officers who come off shift spooked, saying an officer came from nowhere or that a mysterious person gave them a warning only to disappear.

Something Evil Came

My mother was an LPN for 35 years, and she witnessed a lot of things during those years. She told me several stories, but one that sticks out is something that happened during the graveyard shift at a state-run hospital.

One night, a patient was dying and kept screaming "He's coming to get me. Please don't let him take me." They finally calmed her down, and the patient rested soundly after being sedated. Or so they thought.

Within a matter of minutes, a rotten smell permeated the room, and the room got very hot. The thermostat was set at 70 degrees, but the gauge said it was 95. All of a sudden, the patient sat straight up in bed, let out one loud, terrifying scream, and then fell over dead! Once that happened, the rotten smell disappeared within a few minutes, and the temperature dropped back down to the thermostat setting.

A maintenance man checked the thermostat the next morning and said there was nothing wrong with it. My mother was a Christian who had no doubt that something evil came for the dying woman that night. She said the look of sheer terror in the poor dying woman's eyes convinced her that what this woman experienced was all too real.

Haunted Hospital Room

I used to work at this hospital on a pediatric/med-surgery floor. None of the staff liked to go into Room 228. We'd hear disembodied voices and what sounded like a bedside table moving, plus the call light would go off by itself. We tried not to put patients in that room because of the activity.

Not only did us nurses experience activity, but the patients reported activity as well. Some saw a person standing in the corner, while others heard singing. There were also reports of the bed shaking and the bedside table moving. However, the creepiest thing that ever happened was when a child was assigned to Room 228.

One time, a patient's mom stepped off the floor, and I heard the child having a conversation with someone. I went back to the room, and I got chilled. The room felt like it was covered in a thick patch of fog. I asked the child who he was talking to, and he said a lady was talking to him. I left the room feeling a little uneasy and went back to the nurses' station. The mom came back up and went to the room. She then came out said,

"Thanks for having that lady stay with him while I was gone." I just smiled. I wasn't going to tell her that her child was being watched by a ghost.

Somewhere Else

I'm a CNA (certified nursing assistant), and as everyone in the medical field will probably tell you, it's not the easiest job in the world.

Halfway through my certification training, I started hands-on training for my clinical hours at a retirement home in Brunswick, GA. The first day was normal enough, but the second day was something else entirely.

I had just arrived and realized a patient needed assistance via the call light monitor. So I went to see what the problem was.

As soon as I stepped into the patient's room, I realized a few things were a little off. The bed was stripped, there was no name tape or supplies anywhere to be found, no personal items anywhere, and all the shelves were empty. There was nothing but a chair by the window, and there the patient quietly sat. I knew her name because there was an ID slip posted on the door, but for the sake of this story I'll call her Elsa due to HIPPA restrictions.

"Ms. Elsa?" I called her name a few times to no avail. This wasn't unusual as a lot of our patients suffer from Alzheimer's. But there was an unusual stillness about her that made me uneasy. She didn't even appear to be breathing. "Are you ok?" I asked. She didn't answer. I asked her what her favorite food was and if she had any children. Still no answer. She only continued to sit there, staring out of the window.

To gauge the patient's awareness, I asked if she knew where she was. This time she answered back so suddenly it kind of startled me. "Somewhere else," Ms. Elsa replied, a little above a whisper.

I didn't know what that meant at the time, but I do now. I left the room and went to another CNA and asked about Ms. Elsa's condition after telling her what happened. She looked at me for a few seconds and very angrily said that I wasn't funny.

As you can imagine, I was very confused. So I went to the charge nurse for clarity. Upon mentioning Ms. Elsa, her eyes got very wide and she told me "That's impossible, young man. Ms. Elsa died two days ago."

This experience shook me to the core and still does whenever I think about it.

Sounds in the Night

Before my mother died of lung cancer, she suffered in our living room. My dad got a hospital bed from somewhere, and that's where she stayed, getting her morphine.

At night, my mother often felt incredible pain and cried. Because of that, my father ordered us to keep our doors open and wake him up when she cried so that he could take care of her. However, when my mom got weaker, her crying was not loud enough to reach upstairs to our rooms. So, my father got a little stick which was made out of some kind of light wood. When my mother hit the stick against her bed frame, it was loud and clear, and we could hear her.

That time was the worst of my life. Imagine the psychological torture of hearing your mother crying and suffering all the time. It was especially bad when she had had her dose of morphine, but still suffered. Then, my dad told us to ignore her because we couldn't do anything and she would soon go to sleep.

Some days before she passed, my mother cried and suffered even louder, and sleeping was more difficult. By then, we had to ignore her crying most of the time. My sister slept on the sofa in my bedroom because my older brother and his wife moved in temporarily to support my father. They stayed until a few weeks after my mother's death.

One day, I had had enough of this depressing version of *Full House*, and I stayed at my cousin's home over the weekend. After hours of playing video games, my cousin and I went to sleep. That night was the night my mother finally lost her fight against the cancer.

One or two days after her death, I came back home. That's when the creepy stuff started. Since my mother was dead, I was glad to close the door of my room again because I am one of those people who doesn't like to sleep with an open door. But my sister wanted the door to stay open. I was annoyed but left the door open. Shortly after that, I fell asleep.

I don't know what time it was, but I remember waking up to the sound of my mother slamming her wooden stick against the bed frame. It was loud and clear. I thought I had just lost my mind during that stressful time. But then, through the dark, I heard my sister asking if I heard the banging. That's when I got really scared. I ignored her, hoping that she would stop asking. But she kept asking. Then I shouted at my sister, insisting that there was nothing, that it was her imagination and that she needed to shut up because I was trying to sleep. Later, I heard my mother crying, just like she had when she was alive and suffering.

I think that lasted a few days. This is where my memory gets strangely blurry. I can still recall the sound of the stick slamming the bed frame, but when I try to remember how long it lasted, and if my mother was crying more or slamming more, my memory gets foggy. I remember lying in bed at night, my eyes closed, both waiting for the banging and dreading it. However, a few days after my mother's death, the sounds stopped. But not for long...

Now, I hear banging sounds coming from the living room at night. Since my dad sleeps on the couch in the living room, I often tell myself that it is him making the noise. But then again, the banging happens even when he my dad isn't home. I thought I was the only person who heard the banging, but my girlfriend noticed it one night. I told her it was something outside. If I told her the truth, she would never come over again.

I've never told anyone this story. I was 16 when my mother died. I am 25 now. When I hear the noises, I often imagine going downstairs and telling my mom that I love her and apologizing for letting her cry alone because I was too scared to help. I would thank her for everything. I still miss her so much. But the idea of seeing my dead mother is too frightening.

Dead Ringer

My son Jason passed away last July. He was 29 years old, and his death was unexpected. He had recently discharged from the army and had been residing with me for 15 months. I found him in his room when I opened the door. I had so many unanswered questions.

Recently, I was sleeping in the living room because my five-year-old grandson was spending the night. We didn't go to bed until 5 a.m., and I awoke to my cell phone ringing. The phone wasn't near me. It was over on the kitchen table, so I didn't make it to the phone in time to answer. When I picked it up, I expected to see my other son's name, thinking he was checking in to see if my grandson was up yet. However, when I looked at the phone it said I had a missed call from Jason.

The call was from his phone number, and the phone said there was a voice mail. So, with shaking hands, I called back. But there was nothing, just dead silence. I said hello and there was no response. The line stayed open until I finally hung up.

My son's cell phone has been disconnected for 11 months now and sits in my drawer. Even if someone else was given his number, they certainly wouldn't have his contact list to get my number.

I am a big-time skeptic, never believing ghost stories, but I have no explanation whatsoever. I told my other grown children and my daughter even came over to see the number for herself on my missed call list. This happened at exactly 7:02 a.m.

I don't know how, or why, but I would love to believe it was my son calling me from heaven. He is still in my contact list, but the ringer I had assigned to him was not the ring I heard.

I Love You

I was stationed at Fort Stewart, GA. I lived in an apartment with my husband off post in Hinesville.

When we moved into the apartment, the bathroom had long, dark hairs in the tub and sink and a woman's bra behind the door. We didn't think anything of it. We just cleaned our new bathroom and set up house.

During the night, as we slept, the house was silent and there was no disturbance except a sudden chill around two in the morning. This was a little odd since it was a good 85 – 90 degrees outside. In the morning, there were again long, black hairs all over the bathroom. This happened a few days in a row.

One morning we woke up and there was also lipstick on the mirror, scrawled out to say "I love you" and what appeared to be blood drips above the shower. I don't own any makeup, and I moved the bed to the living room after that. The hair stopped showing up, but the blood drips continued for another couple of weeks, along with the lipstick message.

I was becoming increasingly uneasy and moody. Before I moved out, one of our neighbors told us a young lady had killed herself in the bathroom after her husband was deployed and broke up with her for someone in his unit.

I had never been so happy to be moving in my life.

Things That Linger

After my husband and I bought our first home, strange things happened right away. In fact, the activity started our first night there.

We were exhausted from moving, so my parents watched our baby. Soon after crawling into bed, I heard what sounded like a huge party going on in the kitchen. I heard dishes rattling, chairs moving, silverware clanking, etc. After about 45 minutes, I finally rolled over and asked my husband if he heard the sounds. He admitted that he did.

When we got up and opened the bedroom door, the noises stopped. The kitchen was completely silent. We walked around the house and the yard but found nothing. However as soon as we laid back down, the noises resumed. This time we could hear people whispering.

It's amazing what you can get used to. We started sleeping with a fan so we wouldn't hear the noises coming from the kitchen. Other strange things happened, too, like plugs being yanked from sockets.

We lived together for six years, but things didn't work out between me and my husband, and I eventually left with our daughter. Things got worse after that. My ex is now afraid to leave the bedroom without a fully loaded pistol because at night it sounds like someone is trying to break into the home. He says the noises have become more violent. There is also a ghost, a little girl, we've seen around the house. She's been following my ex.

That house changed both our lives. There are things that linger...spiritually.

Water Walker

In Texas, there's a lakeside park called Hunter Park. One night, when I was about 12, we went camping out there. It was me, my brother Cody, my mom, and her boyfriend. Cody claims to have seen something that night that I can't explain.

The two of us were fishing really late at night. I went to bed at about midnight. Cody says that about an hour later he was pulling in his lines so he could also go to sleep. When he looked up, he saw a man in the water about 10 feet away. He said the man was standing ON the water. This person was dressed like a cowboy from what he remembers of it.

The man looked right at him, and Cody said it seemed like the man didn't know he was there. The man looked straight through him. Cody calmly, but quickly, reeled in his line and walked up to the car where I was. He woke me up, trying to tell me he'd just seen something. I was asleep and thought he was messing with me, so I mumbled something and went back to sleep.

The next morning I woke up, and he was telling my mom the same thing. He was really freaked out about it. She didn't believe him at first, but he had way too many details and was way too consistent to be making it up. She finally started to believe him a little.

We later went through some old information in the library and learned that a cattle rustler had drowned in the area back in the late 1890s, before the lake existed. We even found a sketch of a man matching Cody's description.

Did my brother see a ghost? What did this man want with him? Did he even know that we were there? I've thought about this off and on for 15 years.

Yosemite Spirit

It was the summer of 1994. I was a seasonal employee of Yosemite National Park and was housed in a residence near the base of Yosemite Falls in Yosemite Valley. There were several of us housed there, and we all felt that something was watching us. At times, I noticed movement in the corner of my eye, but when I looked, nothing was there.

My room was at the end of a hallway, with a door on one side that led up to a second story by way of stairs. That door was kept locked since nobody was allowed on the second story. One night, my car alarm went off, and I moved through the dark house to disable the alarm. I had no difficulty moving through the dark hallway going out, but coming back to my bedroom, I ran smack into the stairway door that for some inexplicable reason was now open across the hallway. Rubbing my forehead ruefully, I closed the door and climbed back into bed.

Within a minute or two, the same hallway door slammed open and a thumping noise came from the stairway behind it. I stayed in bed. The next day, I was telling my story to a friend in my room when the closet door unlatched by itself and opened fully, emitting a loud, squeaking sound.

This residence is still in the Valley residential area where all the housing was built over the primal sites of Ahwahnichee villages and graveyards. Coincidence? I think not.

Terror on the Farm

This ordeal turned a very religious, anti-paranormal family into stern believers. Here it goes:

This happened between 1986 and 1987. My father bought a farm in the Free State province of South Africa which the locals called Gapamadi. It's Sotho for "the place where the blood flows." The first week or so, everything went without incident. I was about three at the time, so this story is partly what I remember and mostly what I've been told.

Unearthly Knocks

Around the third night on the new farmstead, there came a knock at the master bedroom window. My dad opened the curtain to find no one there. Just as he got into bed, the knock came again, but this time from the kitchen at the other end of the house. My dad got up, but again found on one there. As he turned his back on the door, all hell broke loose. The knocking started again but went in rapid succession, from one window to the other, covering the whole house. As my dad gathered all of us together, it suddenly started hailing STONES!!!!

It went on like this for the rest of the night, until the first African Plovers started their calls in the morning. Then all went silent. Apparently, it did not only torment us as the owners of the farm. The farm workers who were left the next morning didn't want to start work out of fear for the tokoloshe (a sort of household spirit). They believed it was responsible for the phenomenon. Most workers left that same day.

A Glimpse Into the Past

Things slowly escalated from there, as if testing my parent's tolerance. Many times I called for my mom while playing, bathing, etc., telling her to make the "uncle" leave, only for her to find no one around!

Other spirits also started appearing around the house and garden. I believe that these were former owners and inhabitants of our farm. They appeared to be wearing clothes from the early 1900s. An older gentleman in his sixties haunted the house, smoking a pipe (the smell of pipe smoke would sometimes fill the living room) with a young man around his early thirties. On bright, sunny days, we'd see a woman in her thirties cutting roses in the formal garden. A young girl around five years old ran around her mother, both of them wearing bonnets as was the custom among Boer-folk for centuries.

A few nights later, my family heard the neighing of horses in the old stone kraal (corral). There was the sound of hooves on the ground, the muted voices of men talking or discussing something, and the sound of the heavy iron gates swaying open, followed by a voice calling "Voorwaarts, manne!" It roughly translates from Dutch to "Charge, men!" The "horses" would then bolt from the open gates, circling the house, accompanied by the sound of horsewhips. This usually lasted around 30 minutes every night. The creepy part is that the kraal was used by the Boers during the Anglo Boer war of 1899. There are also some British graves in the middle of one of the cornfields as reminder of a Boer victory during some unnamed battle in 1900.

Dog Trouble

One day, my mother cried out in fear. Our healthy Boerboel dogs were lying on their backs with their eyes turned back in their sockets, their mouths foaming. At first, my parents thought the animals had been poisoned. My father fetched the pick-up, put the dogs on the back, and rushed towards town to take them to a vet. Just as my father exited the gate at the border of the farm, the dogs suddenly got up and acted as if nothing was wrong. This continued countless times with the dogs immobilized for up to 15 minutes!

Brother Attacked

Things quickly got worse from this point on. The sound of stones raining on the corrugated roof got worse, and the entity started finding human targets. My father and my 17-year-old brother were on the patio one evening when a stone hit my brother on the forehead. My father and brother both described the sound as a high-pitched whizzing noise, as if the stone had been hurled from a slingshot. The next day, my father installed powerful spotlights around the house and cut all of the lovely fruit trees surrounding the home down in an attempt to catch the culprits. It was all to no avail! Everything continued as usual with no one in sight. It seemed as if the rocks being thrown materialized from thin air.

At this stage, the activity started to focus on my brother. He stayed in his own one-bedroom flat about 10 meters from the main house. One night, he was studying for a year-end exam when something unseen attacked him from behind. My brother was big and strong and into body building at that time, but an epic struggle ensued with the creature trying to strangle him for 25 minutes. When my brother finally broke loose from the creature's grip, he was covered in blood and looked like he'd been strangled with a garrote wire. His chest looked like it had been slashed by claws or blunt metal blades. Now in his forties, my brother still bears the scars on his chest.

The Hellhound

My brother was not the only victim. My mom was lying on the bed one day, reading a book, when she suddenly became paralyzed. Shortly thereafter, a bulldog appeared at the bedroom door. My mother said it felt like eternity as she soaked in every detail of the entity. It also was a Boerboel dog, but he had a white spot between his eyes, whereas ours had black masks. Its face was tinted reddish pink, as if by blood, and red slime dripped from its mouth. The dog then started towards her, jumping on the bed, pinning her down, and staring into her in the eyes. After what must have felt like an eternity, the dog jumped off and left the room. This happened a few times more, even at night with my father next to her. Being paralyzed, my mother could not alert my father.

An Aunt Investigates

Being a stout Protestant Christian, my aunt did not believe the accounts she heard from my mother, so she came to visit with my niece who was around 15 at the time. My sister and my niece were sitting in the bath when a stone flew through the window and cracked the tub between them. My aunt decided to brave the night and sleep over, but when we woke up the next morning, my aunt and niece were gone. They'd packed their bags in the middle of the night and drove the nearly 400 km home. I actually admire her for her bravery as she had to go outside and walk the 20 meters to her car. She said something happened in the spare bedroom shortly after she switched off the lights, but she refuses to tell us what happened to this very day.

Things Get Worse

Although the activity usually started around dusk and continued until the first African Plovers called in the early morning hours, activity started to happen during daylight hours as well. There would be whispering around the house as two dark shadows moved around. These same two dark shadows also circled the house every night. We believed that they were the cause for the poltergeist-like activity. It is actually reported by the natives that tokoloshes usually work in pairs!

At this point, the only time the activity ceased was when the police or people who did not have a close bond to the family visited. It immediately resumed after they left. Around this time, spontaneous fires started around the employees' homes. It started out almost harmless, but one day some of the employees came bashing at the door, screaming that a worker's house was burning down and that flames were leaping from the windows. The worker was on leave and the door was locked from the outside with a strong deadbolt. When they finally opened the door, witnesses saw that only the edges of the kitchen cupboards were burning. After the flames were extinguished and all of the smoke subsided, they were shocked to find that there was NO damage apart from the burst windows and smoke damage.

The Witchdoctor Arrives

My parents were now desperate as my father had put all of their savings into a deposit for the farm. Selling it then would have financially ruined them. The church did not seem to care and even alleged that my parents did this for attention. My parents used to be respected people in town as my father was head of the traffic department and a deacon in church. Suddenly, people laughed behind their backs and most in town had abandoned my family at this stage. Some even accused my brother of staging it all. My dad now was being fed up of nothing working and contacted a traditional African witch doctor from the old Bophuthatswana.

When the witch doctor came, he asked for a glass of water, looked into it, and told my father things of a very personal nature, things very few people knew – certainly no one in town knew. The witch doctor started to perform a cleansing ritual before he removed a few boxes filled with stuff like fingernail clippings, hair, etc. He then went on to tell my dad that the previous owner had put a curse on the farm as he was pissed off because he went bankrupt and wanted no one else to stay for long. The night after the cleansing, a storm came up, but instead of thunder there was the crying of a baby...very freaky! The wind blew from one border fence of the farm to the other, about 1500 hectares, and then almost everything stopped as suddenly as it had started. Most people don't believe my story, but trust me, sometimes the truth really is stranger than fiction.

A Haunted House Turned Haunted Hotel

My family and I lived at a haunted property called Gladstone Villa in the former mining town of Bargoed in the South Wales Valleys during the 1970s. We experienced phenomena that simply defied rational explanation like footsteps in the bedroom when we would all be downstairs watching TV.

Living on the property were my grandparents, my mother, and me. My dad left home in 1972 when I was three years old, and my parents eventually divorced. My mother told me the noises started off in the attic soon after I was born and eventually moved into the main bedroom, which was my grandparents' room. We would hear the noises, which sounded like someone walking about the bedroom, every evening, sometimes during the day.

A Medium's Visit

A family friend, Mrs. France, who would visit the family every evening, did not believe my grandmother at first when she told her it was haunted, saying that the noises were caused by vibrations from the traffic outside. However, one evening she had her belief system challenged when she experienced the noises for herself. She suggested contacting the local press, but my grandmother refused for fear of ridicule.

Mrs. France said she knew of a medium, and he eventually came to Gladstone Villa. At first, the medium began by asking questions. He then started challenging the entity to perform by knocking on the ceiling to see if he would get a reaction. Sure enough, the spirit promptly knocked back at him! At one point, the medium went into a trance to try and make contact. He didn't get a name, but he later confirmed the obvious: that there was indeed a presence in the house. He said it was an earthbound spirit.

A priest was also called, and he blessed the property, and he said some prayers, and it was quiet for a few short months. However, the spirit returned with a vengeance and this time decided to show itself.

The Hooded Monk and the Old Man

One evening, my mother, grandfather, and I were watching TV. My grandmother was reading a book on the settee when my mother just happened to look towards her and see the figure of a monk standing behind the sofa near the door way. We didn't see the figure as we were watching TV, but she later described it as a figure with typical monk's garb and a hood covering the face. There were more sightings after that, and the noises continued.

One afternoon, I remember my mother going towards the settee to get something when she looked to her left, toward an open door that led to the hallway. I saw the expression on her face, one of confusion, as if she had seen someone. She told me she saw an old man with white hair looking into the living room. She said it was a face she didn't know.

Poltergeist Activity

There was also some minor poltergeist activity. I recall one day my grandfather coming into the living room from upstairs with a broken bottle. He said it was thrown towards him, just missing him. I didn't actually witness this, but I'm inclined to believe him. There were more incidents, but we didn't hear strange sounds all the time. When we did, we would turn the TV down to hear the sounds more clearly. It sounded like someone walking about in the bedroom. My grandfather would try to point out exactly where it was by saying "He's by here," "He's by there now." We had the ghost for so long that my grandmother gave it a name. She called him Johnny. My grandfather would sometimes mock the spirit by shouting "Johnny-o."

The Haunted Redz Parc Hotel

We left Gladstone Villa in June 1978, after two local business men bought the property. It was eventually converted into a hotel and is now called Redz Parc Hotel. I had my 40th birthday there for old time's sake, and the staff told me of the ghost before I said anything. I told them I lived there in the 1970s, and they told me of their own experiences. Johnny the Ghost is still there! Apparently, there have been sightings in Room 5.

What I have said here is true, and I wouldn't say it if I couldn't possibly back it up with evidence. My family, and the staff at Redz Parc Hotel, and the people that stayed there cannot all be lying. My grandmother sadly passed away in 1982, but my mother, my grandfather, and I still remember the haunting and wouldn't want to go through all that again.

The Man in the Dunes

This happened at night at Tybee Island Beach in Georgia. Three of my friends and I were smoking on the beach, looking towards the dunes. There was a heat lightning storm that was going crazy right over Tybee. While we were sitting on the beach, we all noticed a man-shaped shadow in the dunes.

We sat smoking and discussing whether it was a man or a tree. After several minutes of observing, we came to the conclusion that it was a tree or bush shaped like a man because there was absolutely no movement over a period of 15-20 minutes.

We decided to go look for ourselves. On the approach, all the classic ghost story shit happened...change of temperature, hairs on the back of the neck and arms standing up, mood changes. We all went from curious, to terrified, before we even got close.

Once we were within about 15 to 20 feet of the thing, a giant bolt of heat lightning struck and lit up the night sky like it was daytime. All of the power went out on Tybee. For that split second of light, we all saw him: a fully transparent man in homemade clothing. We could clearly see the features on his face. He stood there not looking at us, not moving at all. He had a blank face like a little kid watching cartoons. We were all so scared. We all screamed and ran. We didn't even look back.

I've talked with different ghost hunters since then, and they pointed out key elements in the experience such as the heat lightning. They say that whatever these things are can get their power from electricity in the atmosphere.

Anyway, that's my true ghost story. What do you think?

Haunted House on the Hill

I service pools for a living, and there's one house I visit that really gives me the creeps. The house is huge, a mansion really, but it's been empty for awhile. The bank or someone pays the pool bill to keep the house marketable, but I don't think they'll sell it anytime soon. This is in Deer Creek, Oklahoma.

I've been to the house close to a hundred times, and I almost always see shadows in the windows. Like I said, the house is locked up and empty, but there's always something going on in the windows. My crew and I also hear barking dogs, though there's no dogs on the property and the house is on a hill far from anything else. The dogs sound close too. Another time, I heard something banging on an upstairs window, but when I turned around no one was there. On a different day, I swear I heard someone whisper "What's your name?".

The worst was when the pool's pump motor quit working for no reason. I was flipping breakers, cussing and yelling, when the motor suddenly kicked on and I heard loud clapping coming from the house. I hauled ass out of there that day.

Other people who work at the house have told me they've heard people dancing upstairs and seen doors fling upon by themselves. The caretaker often has to check on the house in the middle of the night because the alarm system registers doors opening and closing.

I don't know a whole lot about the history of the house, or the land it sits on, but the story is that an oil worker was killed on the property sometime in the 1950s. Maybe that's who's bumping around that big, empty house.

The Couple Trapped in Time

In 1990 or 1991, I lived with my family in a small town in West Virginia. We had just moved into a rental house, one the owner guessed to be over a hundred years old. While there, everyone in my family – my ex and I, our two teenage sons, our 8-year-old daughter, and our two toddler sons – experienced something strange.

The first strange thing we noticed was an occasional cold spot near the bathroom door. Later, we heard bumps and the occasional thud and sometimes an object would move around or disappear. For example, we'd leave a pen on a table and it would turn up in a completely different spot. We also heard footsteps which we could track because of the creaky floors.

One time I was in the basement when I heard what sounded like a chest of drawers tumbling down the stairs. Everyone in the house heard the crash and came running from all directions to see what had fallen. However, after searching the home we couldn't find anything wrong.

Though we didn't have any of the usual haunted house stuff – strange smells, whispers in the night, shadows lurking in the corner – we all knew something was off. We didn't think we were in any danger, however, so we accepted the strange events and went on with our daily lives.

The eerie happenings seemed to increase in duration the longer we lived there, and they seemed to be focused on men. One night, I was sitting on the edge of my bed, taking off my shoes, when I felt something strange. Looking up, I saw a woman floating in the hallway. She was wearing old-fashioned clothing, like something you'd see in the 1800s, and just hovered above the floor, staring at me. She was frozen, yet alive. Solid, not transparent. Strangely, the woman seemed like a photo. She did not seem to fit into our world.

I just knew she was waiting for me to make a move, so I did. I said: "So you're the one who's in the house, doing all these things." About 20 seconds later, the woman did a ninety-degree turn and floated off towards the kitchen. She made no sound and didn't move her body at all. She simply floated away. I didn't pursue her. I just took off my shoes and went to bed.

The next day, I told my family what happened and we all just accepted the weird event and moved on. However, the next day, right at the same time, I looked up and saw a man in the hallway. He was also wearing old clothes, though he stood on the floor instead of floating over it. Like the ghost woman from the night before, the man had no expression on his face, and he seemed frozen and out of place.

I did the same thing I did the night before. I spoke to the entity, saying something like: "So you must be the man of the house, the husband of the woman I saw last night." At first, he didn't move, but 20 seconds later he disappeared completely. He looked like a series of dots blinking out. Gone. The next day, I told my family, and they once again accepted the story and moved on. We weren't afraid, just a little concerned about whatever was in the house.

The man and woman never appeared again. No one saw anything at all, although we continued to hear footsteps, creaking boards, and the occasional bumps and thuds. However, I can say no objects moved or disappeared again.

Today, looking back, I think the ghosts, or whatever they were, just wanted to be noticed. They were like a memory, a residual, with some degree of intelligence. I think they were something "stuck in time," living there in a loop of sorts, not sure what to do next.

Jeremy

This happened when I was about 16. My best friend and I were on a summer trip with her grandmother. While in Oklahoma, we were staying at her grandmother's vacation house. It was our first night there, and my friend and I were in the guest bedroom on our cots. Her grandmother and sister were sleeping down the hall in the master bedroom.

For some reason, I could not go to sleep. I sometimes get creeped out in new places, but I also kept thinking I heard someone walking on the gravel driveway next to the house. I could hear a voice, but not clearly. It sounded to me like the voice was calling someone, and I heard the name Jeremy. I figured it was just a neighbor looking for their pet, but it still weirded me out a little since it was around 3:00 in the morning.

Then I heard banging in the kitchen, like cabinet doors being shut. At this point, I was majorly creeped out so I woke up my friend. She was kind of annoyed at first, but once I told her what I had heard she grew wide awake and started getting creeped out too. We sat there for a few minutes, not hearing anything else, just talking and giggling and basically being teenage girls.

After a few minutes, my friend said she had to go to the bathroom, but at this point she was too scared to go by herself. So we both stood up to leave. The second our feet hit the floor, we heard pounding footsteps running down the hall towards our door. This was one of those houses that's raised off the ground, so the steps were very loud. We flew back onto the cots, and the sounds stopped. We sat there for about 15 minutes, huddled up on the same cot, laughing uneasily and wondering what the hell just happened. My friend still needed to go to the bathroom (a little more urgently now), so after a couple of minutes of gathering our courage we climbed off the cot.

Again, the split second our feet touched the floor, the pounding footsteps came running down the hall. This time we totally lost it and started screaming our heads off. We jumped back onto the cot, which promptly collapsed under our weight, and sat there on the floor, tangled up in blankets and a broken cot, screaming bloody murder. We didn't hear anymore footsteps, though I'm not sure if they stopped the second we jumped on the cot like before. We were screaming too loud.

While we were shrieking, the door to our room opened, making us scream louder, but it was just my friend's grandmother wondering what on earth was wrong. We told her about the footsteps, but she just told us we were being silly and gave us that old line about there wasn't anything in the dark that wasn't also in the light. Then we told her about what had kept me awake in the first place - the steps outside, the voice, the cabinets - but she was shrugging it off until I said that I'd heard the name Jeremy.

At that point, she shot my friend a very strange look and asked her how I knew about Jeremy. My friend asked what she meant (she didn't know anything about a Jeremy either). Turns out, Jeremy was the grandson of the man that used to live in the house (both relatives of my friend's grandmother) and that they had had a falling out and hadn't made up when the man died.

At that point, I think her grandmother believed us a bit more. However, she didn't really say much, just that Jesus was always watching over us and that we should go back to sleep. My friend also got up and went to the bathroom (finally) and there were no steps that time. Nothing else happened during that visit, or any others, but we didn't get much sleep either. I guess the ghost of that man is still looking for his grandson, trying to patch things up.

The Man with the Pearl Buttons

I was 15 years old when I had my very first encounter with a ghost. It was on a late spring morning. My parents were at work, and my brothers and sister were either off with their friends or running errands.

One of my chores for the day was to vacuum the living room. I love the smells of spring and the sound of birds chirping, so I opened the windows and front door to air out the house. I started vacuuming, and about two minutes into the job, I caught a glimpse of a rather tall man standing in the doorway. He was balding on top, with white hair on the sides, wearing a red shirt with pearl buttons.

I turned off the vacuum cleaner off and started towards the door when I noticed there was no one there. Panic set in when I thought, "He came into the house!" I was all alone and there was a strange man in the house. Being a 15-year-old female, we tend to be dramatic. I screamed at the top of my lungs! A neighbor who was outside sweeping his sidewalk came running over to see what was going on.

I asked the neighbor if he'd seen the man who came into my house. The neighbor said he'd been outside for a while and didn't see anyone come up to our door. I told him that the man must be in the house, so we went from room to room to see if we could find him. There was no one in the house. When my parents came home, I told them what happened and they went over to the neighbor's house to talk with him about the incident.

Later that evening, when my mother and I were cooking dinner, my mother told me she had seen the man several times before and that he was a ghost. I didn't say anything. I just stayed quiet because I didn't know which one of us was crazy, or if we both were.

Seven years later, my parents decided to tear down an old building that had been on the property since 1910. Under the floorboards, they found a skeleton, some pearl buttons, and old coins. They had to call the police who then got the coroner's office involved. They discovered that the skeleton was that of a man who was probably a homesteader before New Mexico was a state.

My dad reminded me of what happened when I was 15. He said, "I guess you saw this man's ghost."

Evil Dolls

Weird things started happening to me about a year ago. I moved into a new unit in Brisbane, QLD, and got my porcelain dolls back from my mother's place. I've had the dolls since I was 5 years old. Everyone used to tell me they were evil, but I didn't believe them.

I put the seven dolls away in a box and left them in the spare room. I then began having nightmares, starting with one or two a week. After a while, they started to occur every single night. I've never experienced nightmares like this in my life. These were full on extreme night terrors. I didn't understand what was going on and was exhausted all the time from lack of sleep.

I then started to hear some kind of scratching noise coming from inside the closet or from just outside my room late at night – never during the day. At the time, I thought it might be a mouse. These things happened for a couple of months.

One time I was sitting in the lounge room, watching TV, when all of a sudden I saw two small, red eyes on the side of my cat's body when he sitting on my lap. They were just staring at me. I looked behind me to see where it was coming from and saw nothing but a blank wall. I looked back and the eyes were still there. Then they slowly faded away.

On another occasion, I was lying in bed and had the outside hall light on, when I saw a murky, dark shadow come across the ceiling and into my room. It then disappeared. The last thing that happened before I spoke to someone about the weird events was when I saw a demonic-looking face in the reflection of the base of my lamp. It was staring at me. The thing had dark circles as eyes, and it wasn't clear like a human face, but it was definitely a face.

I eventually spoke to a lady at work, a Jehovah's Witness, about everything that happened, and she told me that I had something in my house that was causing the problems. I didn't fully believe it was the dolls at the time, but I ended up throwing them out in the industrial bin that weekend because something needed to happen to make it stop. The dolls were worth hundreds of dollars, but I was not risking it. That night, I had an extreme nightmare about them. The dolls were at my Nan's house, where they had been originally, and they had killed my cat. In the dream, I found his body in the kitchen sink.

It's been over nine months now, and I've had no nightmares, no weird noises, or feelings of another presence. I feel stronger and healthier, and I always pray from time to time, asking the lord to protect me and Hugo (my cat). Everything stopped after I threw out those dolls. I now know not to ignore things and to become more in touch with my spiritual side. And I will never buy my daughter a porcelain doll!

Mannequin Shenanigans

I work at a Dillard's in Florida, and there's a possessed mannequin in my department.

This particular mannequin stands near the front of the department, by one of the main entrances, and we use it to display dresses and gowns (I work in juniors). It's always creeped me out. I feel like it's constantly watching me. We have two or three other mannequins in the department, but this one just feels wrong.

One night, right before closing, I was straightening a rack of clothes near the mannequin when I heard a loud scraping sound. Only one other person was working with me that night, but she was downstairs returning a pair of shoes. I thought someone else had come to drop something off, but when I turned around, I saw that the mannequin was facing AWAY from the entrance instead of towards the door like it normally does. I won't lie. After seeing that, I ran to the other end of the department and refused to move until my co-worker came back.

A few weeks later, I came into work for a morning shift and found the mannequin in one of the dressing rooms. I was pretty freaked to find it there, but assumed one of my co-workers had moved it. Soon after that, a member of the visual team came by and wanted to know where the mannequin was. I told her it was in the dressing room. She got pretty mad because apparently the night before, she'd dressed the mannequin in one of our expensive gowns and had created a prom-themed display. I asked around, but everyone denied moving the mannequin.

I'm not the only one who's had an experience. My co-worker Rebecca was walking by the mannequin one night when she heard someone hiss, "Leeaave." She swears the mannequin also turned its head, but I can't verify that. Another time, a customer was checking out the price tag on a dress the mannequin was wearing when she felt a shock, like she had been electrocuted. She actually shrieked pretty loudly, and my manager rushed over to see what was wrong. He's heard all about the mannequin, but doesn't believe there's anything to the stories.

The latest, and perhaps creepiest thing, happened this week. A few days ago, one of our customers lost a locket while trying on clothes. She was really upset because her dad and given her the locket, and he's since passed away. We looked all over the dressing room, and all around the department, but didn't find it anywhere. The girl left crying, and I felt really bad, but I didn't know what else to do. Last night I walked by the mannequin and found the damn locket hanging around its neck! Even more disturbing, the locket was empty. The picture that had been inside was gone.

14963444R00025

Printed in Poland
by Amazon Fulfillment
Poland Sp. z o.o., Wrocław